31 Tips to Enhancing Your Personal Praise-Dance Ministry

Improve Within A Month!

Stephanie Esters

Purposed Publishing 8:18

31 Tips to Enhancing Your Personal Praise-Dance Ministry:
Improve Within a Month!

All rights reserved.

No portion of this book may be shared, photocopied or otherwise reproduced, communicated or transmitted via any social media platform or stored on any retrieval system or device, without the written express permission of the author.

Copyright © 2017 by Stephanie Esters
All rights reserved.

First edition 2017

31 Tips to Enhancing Your Personal Praise-Dance Ministry: Improve Within a Month!

ISBN: 978-0-983-8097-2-2

Purposed Publishing 8:18

Printed in the United States of America

Dedication

*To Momma and Daddy,
Teretha & R.L.*

~I finally got it done!

Table of Contents

Dedication

Acknowledgments

Preface

1. Seek God first 1
2. Seek God as your first Choreographer 2
3. Listen to and heed God 3
4. Focus on the lyrics of the song 4
5. Live a life that praises and honors God 5
6. Develop a humble spirit 6
7. Learn biblical themes. 7
8. Minister, not 'perform' your dance 8
9. Articulate your dance! 9
10. Dance big —- bigger still! 10
11. Eradicate the 'Salome' factor 11
12. Videotape for self-critique 12
13. Keep your 'iron' sharp 13
14. Consider your garments 14
15. Learn your colors! 15
16. Use 'praise dance tools.' 16
17. Teach someone else 17
18. Know your spiritual gifting. 18
19. Practice. Practice. Practice! 19
20. Think outside the box. 20
21. Take care of your 'temple.' 21
22. Looking good: Great hygiene and grooming. 23
23. Position yourself for The Anointing. 24
24. Stand tall! 25

25. Take a formal dance class 26
26. Minister with passion! 27
27. "Emote" your facial expressions 28
28. Just flow 29
29. Respect others' ministries 30
30. Fast and pray 31
31. Avoid competition. 32
32. Now What? Take it to the streets! (Evangelism!) 33
33. Notes 34-36
34. Resources 37
35. Bibliography . . . .
    39
36. Index . . . .
    41

Acknowledgements

This book is a compilation of many of the practices I learned and used that helped me enhance my own personal praise-dance ministry, techniques that I was then able to share with others to help them in their ministries.

Here, I want to acknowledge the people who provided encouragement to me along my journey: that anointed young dance ministry from King Solomon M.B. Baptist Church in Metcalfe, Mississippi, that first piqued my interest in worshipping The Lord through dance; one of my first young mentor-sisters in dance, Sis. Jessica Thornton Kreichauf; that enthusiastic youth praise-dance ministry, my first adult praise-dance ministry and my pastor, the Dr. Rev. Addis Moore, all at Mt. Zion Baptist Church in Kalamazoo, Michigan; my first true dance-sister for life, visionary Jasmine Robinson of Leaps of Faith Dance Company; my virtual mentor-teachers, Jocelyn Richard of The Praise Dance Life and Lynn Hayden of Dancing For Him Ministries; and Bianca, Tina and Telia and Pastor Roz and all the other beginning dance ministers who encouraged me by soaking up what I had to teach, allowing me to 'work out my teaching' on them. Then, a special 'thank you' to all those people close to me who 'had to endure' me ~ who had to listen to me talk one more time about 'any and everything praise dance'!

I pray that this work blesses others, as the lessons I learned blessed my own ministry.

Preface

By the time I started 'publicly' praise dancing, I had been a 'private' student of the Word on dance and worship for almost seven years, picking up inspirations wherever I could.

Once I started publicly praise dancing, I still continued being a very eager student, desiring to live a life that pleases God and invites Him to dance with me when I minister!

The tips I listed here are some of the practical steps that I took to improve my personal dance ministry, physically and spiritually. Perhaps there is something within these pages that you might find worth trying — I pray at least one of these 'tips' blesses you!

While you might not be able to accomplish some of these steps within a day, start them anyway and expect the growth and improvements in your personal dance ministry!

. . . and let's see what <u>you</u> look 31 days from now!

"Seek God First"

❧ Tip #1 ☙

If you are looking to enhance your personal praise-dance ministry, start first by focusing on and seeking after God: This cannot be emphasized enough.

This should be the first thing you do, as, prayerfully, it was He Who sent you into this ministry in the first place! Otherwise, if you are dancing without the direction and under the anointing of God, you are 'just dancing,' merely entertaining others. While you might be very talented and skillful at doing it, your dance might lack effect, purpose, the supernatural and anointed ability, through God, of influencing onlookers to make an initial or stronger decision to follow Christ. *You cannot bypass God to get at the "goodies" associated with praise dance!*

The Bible tells us that God is Spirit and that we must worship Him in "spirit and in truth" (John 4:24). The Greek word for 'spirit' is *pneúma,* which refers to breath, breathing and life, according to biblehub.com. He 'breathes' on us, breathing life into us, giving us breathe and Word to move on to others. The Message version of the Bible explains that this way:

> *"It's who you are and the way you live that count before God. Your worship must engage your spirit in the pursuit of truth. That's the kind of people the Father is out looking for: those who are simply and honestly themselves before him in their worship. God is sheer being itself — Spirit. Those who worship him must do it out of their very being, their spirits, their true selves, in adoration."*
>
> ~ *John 4:23-24 (The Message Bible)*

Once we look to God, it is He Who will tell us when to dance, how to dance, why to dance.
We will dance with His Anointing.

"Look to God as Your First Choreographer"

∾ Tip #2 ∾

How often have you listened to lyrics from a song or lines of scripture that you couldn't wait to create a choreography for, only to find yourself stumped for days, weeks, maybe even months as you grappled to come up with the perfect dance moves? Or, maybe you developed a choreography, but when it was presented, you felt in your soul that it was not well-received and less than effective and, simply put, '*fell flat*.'

This could be a small reality check, or a reminder check, that when we say we work for God, we need to be sure to consult Him *first*. If God nestled a song or scripture in your spirit, He will be true to guide you in developing choreography or movement to explain it.

So instead of checking websites or YouTube videos to see how other dancers have interpreted those songs or scriptures in the past, ask God for inspiration! Ask Him what He wants you to do or tell people through the song. Even though your moves and interpretation might not seem as "advanced" as those of others you see, trust that God knows what He's doing. There have been many times when I trusted God for a simple move or gesture that seemed to really 'speak' to people watching. *Let's lean on God, and not on our own understanding, so He will direct our steps — and dance (adapted, Proverb 3:5-6)!*

As you continue listening to God, start saturating yourself with the song or words, repeatedly listening to them so the words will begin to marinate — or, soak — in your heart. Trust that God will start revealing what He wants you to do in your dance ministry. <u>Trust Him!</u>

<u>Keep a notepad and pencil, or phone notepad handy</u>, as God might download to you images and movements for your next dance, while you're busy cleaning or working on something else.

Keeping seeking and be ever attentive!

"Listen and Hear from God . . .
<u>Heed</u> What He Has to Say"

❧ Tip #3 ❧

I sometimes like to think that praise dancers and other worship-arts ministers have the heart of God, as they interpret Word from God to the congregation and other onlookers.

For this to be true means we ministers should be spending quality time "heeding" or listening to the voice of God. I feel compelled to say this starts in private worship and study at home and then extends to faithful worship and Bible study at church, with your Bible-teaching and preaching pastor.

To heed something or someone means *"to pay attention"* or to *"to give consideration or attention to"* or to *"mind"* that thing or person, according to the Merriam-Webster online dictionary. Do we, do you, really heed the voice of the One we call Lord? In Luke 6:46 (NIV), the Lord asks us: *"Why do you call me, 'Lord, Lord,' and do not do what I say?"*

We should strive to be so attuned to the Holy Spirit and so willing to walk in His Will, that we hear him directing us to areas in and outside of our ministry. For instance, He might direct you to use your "art as ministry," taking your dance, mime or drama "to the streets," to places like juvenile homes and nursing homes, places where people are less likely to hear the Word of God. Could He be directing you to create a Christian dance musical, a drama told through music and dance, to evangelize to folks? Could He be directing you to write a book explaining what worship is and why everyone is to do it?

Be obedient and sure to follow through, as obedience is '*better than sacrifice*' (1 Samuel 15:22). As my pastor says, *"Delayed obedience is disobedience."*

"Focus on the Lyrics of the Song, Then Seek Scripture That Applies To It"

～ Tip #4 ～

What song are you working on to minister through choreography or free-form?

What are the lyrics saying? What, then, will your dance movements say? (Free tip: If you're desperately searching a song for Word-based lyrics or Bible themes and coming up empty-handed, you might need to select another song!)

I am amazed sometimes at the instances where someone is working on a song or ministering it and a reference is made to the underlying scripture and that person appears to have no knowledge of what the Word is that's being uplifted. If we dance dances that *"lift up that word,"* then we lift up *'The Word,'* Who draws all people to Himself (John 12:32).

If we don't know what we should be ministering, then we miss the opportunity to minister what God really wants His people to hear and see, to be aware of, to mark ("heed").

So the next time you're ministering to a song or words, be sure to understand and meditate on the scripture that explains it. If you have to, write out the lyrics to the song or find them online and print them out.

When you first learn of the song assignment, listen to it in its entirety. Ask yourself what the song is saying? What scriptures does it refer to or include? What do you perceive God is wanting to communicate to people through your dance? Record your thoughts and reflections in the "Notes" section at the back of this book.

Then, dance the Word in the song!

"Live A Life that Praises and Honors God"

≈ Tip #5 ≈

I'm often reminded of the Biblical account of the sons of Eli, the priest's servants who squandered and abused the people, especially the women, who came before them in the temple with offerings. It seems that God gave their father time after time to take care of his wayward sons, but when Eli was slow to handle his sons' missteps, God Almighty stepped in and executed judgment *Himself! Ouch!* He declared that Eli's blood line would never see its male descendants reach old age and that both of Eli's sons would die on the same day! *(Read the account of Eli's wicked sons in 1 Samuel 2.)*

This should serve as a warning to us that we are to live pure and holy before God and His people and all others to whom He has called us to minister. *Our 'off-the-stage walk and character' must line up with our 'on-stage walk and presentation'!*

We can't commit sinful acts and then act as if no one sees us or knows about our dealings. How horrible does that look on ministry and how much of a stumbling block will that be to others in the church and community?

It's like that old saying — which is really scriptural — that says what's done in the dark will show up in the light. *"For there is nothing hidden that will not be disclosed..."* (Luke 8:17).

God says, *"Those who honor me I will honor, but those who despise me will be disdained (v. 30b) . . . I will raise up for myself a faithful priest, who will do according to what is in my heart and mind. I will firmly establish his house, and he will minister before my anointed one always"* (1 Samuel 2:35).

"Develop A Humble Spirit"

❧ Tip #6 ☙

Dancing is one of those pursuits that typically invites personalities with '*rea*l healthy egos,' with an extra focus on "real." Throw in dance-artists who are skilled, expert and sometimes competitive at what they do, and you can see how we can become a ministry falling victim to pride, hubris.

The Word reminds us that one of the things that God detests is a haughty spirit (*Proverbs 6:17);* it also says that He resists the proud, but exalts *(James 4:10)* and gives grace (unmerited or undeserved favor) to the humble *(James 4:6 and 1 Peter 5:5).*

When we are humbled, God is able to be magnified through us, and we execute ministry that is able to touch another person's soul because we're "bowed down" before The Lord. You might be the least technically skilled person in the ministry, but when God exalts you and your humble spirit, you are able to minister with power.

Think of the one entity in the Bible that was so full of pride that he wanted to take over the heavens and God's Kingdom —- that pride was resisted and eventually kicked out of heaven *(Luke 10:8 and Revelation 12:7-9).*

Let us possess and minister in a humble spirit.

For God says that He will share His Glory with no one.

So as we minister —- and are sure to experience accolades from onlookers —- let us do so with humble hearts and spirits, not thinking of ourselves too highly, lest The One To Whom All Glory Is Due take offense.

"Know Biblical Themes: Sin, Grace, Mercy, Salvation, Hope . . ."

❧ Tip #7 ❧

Many Christian praise and worship songs deal with common themes: sin, grace, mercy, salvation, hope, redemption, love, sacrifice, renewal, humility and the list goes on and on.

As a worship-arts dance minister, you will want to have a basic understanding of what these words mean and know some corresponding scripture. This will help in receiving choreography for your ministry.

For instance, if you are seeking inspiration for choreography for a song about **_redemption,_** know that it means *"to buy something back or to stand in the place of something or someone."* It can also mean *"deliverance or rescue or atonement for guilt,"* according to Dictionary.com.

These are scriptural citations: *"I know that my Redeemer lives"* (John 19:25, NIV); and *"He did not enter by means of the blood of goats and calves; but he entered the Most Holy Place once for all by his own blood, having obtained eternal redemption"* (Hebrews 9:12).

Does this help you better with interpretation and understanding of the songs and scriptures to which you minister? *I pray so!*

Don't wait until you need a song with a certain theme: Create your own list now! I did — view my list at www.tinyurl.com/PraiseDanceThemes.

What song are you currently working on? What is the Biblical theme in that song? List the corresponding scripture. Meditate on these.

Song Title: _____

Theme(s): _____

Scripture(s): _____

"Minister Your Dance, As Opposed to 'Performing' Your Dance"

❧ Tip #8 ☙

There is nothing so soul-stirring as an authentic dance, one that seems to be poured out from the very soul of the dancer. This is an observation that can be made, irrespective of the dancer's skill level and natural talent.

Rev. Christopher M. Moore, an associate minister at my church, makes a statement about general worship that I believe is very apropos for praise-dance ministers. He has said that there is nothing like hearing someone beautifully sing a song, say *"Amazing Grace,"* then hearing another person 'really sing' that song because they've '<u>*experienced*</u>' that 'amazing grace'!

This is not to say that praise-dancers need to have experienced every emotion or pain in every song that they minister to, but they should search themselves to draw upon their own similar experiences or the empathy they've felt for someone in that situation. Meditating on the lyrics and scripture of a song will help with 'ministering' a song.

However, when praise-dancers appear to act out part of a song, as opposed to authentically presenting the song, it can sometimes appear forced or manufactured. One of the most authentic dances I ever witnessed was from a very young girl, who danced with such raw technical skill, but she was so authentic and her ministry so anointed! She of so little skill and technique moved many, many people in the church that revival night with her ministry to Shekinah Glory's song *"Yes"! She definitely <u>ministered</u> that song!*

We have to learn how to tell that story, how to be the 'canvas' that others can look to and read what God is saying: *"Write the vision; make it plain on tablets, so he may run who reads it"* (Habakkuk 2:2, English Standard Version).

"Articulate That Dance!"

❧ Tip #9 ❧

I've been guilty —- *very guilty!* —- of presenting dances with moves that were less-than clear, maybe too rushed, cut off or inappropriate for the words sung.

I believe this is why some former and present cheerleaders can adapt very well to praise dance: They are accustomed and trained to presenting sharp, clear, precise movements; this same precision, when overlaid with more artistic and fluid dance movements, can create very engaging, clear-to-understand choreography and dance messages.

The next time you're creating choreography or practicing a dance, watch your own movements in the mirror or videotape the dance for later review and self-critique.

Are your movements sharp and clear? Are your arms strong and curved or straight (as the needs call for), and well-positioned and not lazy or floppy? Did your legs make a complete, strong fan kick (a raising of the leg in the shape of an arc, like a folding hand fan) and were those other lower body movements sharp and completely executed? Did you cut off a move because you were so intent on executing the next movement? Did you have *too many* moves, leading to a dance that was too 'clouded' with movement?

Try this: Without music, present your dance before someone and see if they can understand what you are dancing or trying to present. Their comments might prove to be very insightful for you. Work on 'articulating' — making clear — your dance!

"Dance B – I – G"

❧ Tip #10 ↢

Sometimes when I'm working with a new dancer, I will tell them to dance "big." They may then make movements that they think are big, but which are not quite what I was looking for, leading me to respond: *"dance even bigger!"*

As a little girl, I can remember my music teacher telling us to sing or speak to the back wall of the elementary school auditorium, which probably had 15 rows of seats. She wanted to ensure that our speech and singing projected, that it reached the person even in the furthest-most back seat of the little auditorium.

The same applies to praise-dancers, in my opinion. When you are dancing, make movements so large that even the person sitting farthest from you, in the back-most corner, will no doubt 'hear' and 'see' what it is you are dancing with your whole body.

While attempting this, you might feel very silly and think onlookers must think you're being very foolish and excessive . . . *'doing too much,'* some young people say. But, if you could see what most onlookers actually see, you might see them actually enjoying a dance whose movements they can clearly 'see' and that they see being clearly interpreted.

So don't be embarrassed or self-conscious . . . go ahead . . . *dance big!*

Got it?

Now . . . dance even . . .

b – i – g – g – e – r !

"Eradicate the 'Salome' Factor"

❧ Tip #11 ❧

There was once a young girl whose stepfather wanted her to dance for his birthday celebration. The young girl's dance made such an impact that her stepfather promised her anything she wanted. *Imagine what kind of dance that must have been!*

Anyway, the girl consulted with her mother, who suggested that the girl ask for the head, on a platter, of one of their nemesis —- the man who had been very critical of the mother's marriage to her former brother-in-law.

That young girl was named Salome and her dance is believed to have been so seductive and powerful that it led her stepfather, Herod, to acquiesce and behead the imprisoned John the Baptist (Matthew 14:61-13). *If you don't know the story, go read it!*

That spirit of Salome is very much at work in some praise-dance ministries. It is a spirit of seductiveness, one that instead of delivering a Word to onlookers actually has the reverse effect. It can cause stir up thoughts of lust among onlookers.

Sometimes, some dances can look just a little bit too sexy — yes, I said it! — presented by dancers wearing form-fitting leotards or knit dresses with no overlay (for modesty's sake, to reduce attention to the breast area). *Don't dance like that!*

Simply put, check yourself to make sure your dance, dress and attitude do not have that 'come-hither' or other sexual undertones (or overtones!) that can cause onlookers to stumble.

Eradicate, or get rid of, that Salome factor!

"Videotape and Self-Critique Your Own Personal Dance Ministry"

~ Tip #12 ~

My personal praise-dance ministry grew by leaps and bounds because of this next tip: videotaping and critiquing your own personal dance.

Because I had such a hard time learning choreography, I started buying DVDs from the Sunday duplication ministry to try and learn the dances. Not really realizing it, I was getting a front-seat to my own ministry presentation and oftentimes what I saw did not please me at all!

It is funny how moves that I thought were seamless in my head could appear idiotic on videotape. *(Yep!)* Critiquing my dance movements helped me to refine my dance. One thing I got rid of was a little bop that I had whenever I danced and especially when I turned. I don't know quite what I was doing to affect that bop, but once I became conscious of it, I got rid of it . . . and then, at least my pirouettes, full turns on the front of one foot, and other turns were a lot smoother.

This is akin to what football coaches do with their teams: they review tapes of games to help players improve their play and strategies.

So, consider videotaping your group or private practice sessions and ministry presentations and personally reviewing them to help you improve. These days, many cell phones have videotaping capabilities that allow you to have almost instant feedback.

The videotape don't lie!!

"Keep Your 'Iron' Sharp: Attend a Conference or Workshop This Year"

❧ Tip #13 ❧

The Bible admonishes us to be excellent in all that we do.
We do that by seeking God for guidance.

In the practical, we can also seek out Godly mentors and ministry-leaders at some of the many praise-dance conferences and workshops held across the country or by accessing some of the many teleconferences and tele-seminars going on at any given time during the week. Many of these, right now, can be accessed for a minimal cost — for the cost of a telephone call.

If you or your group is unable to travel to one, you could also consider inviting one of these leader-teachers to your church or community to share his or her expertise; maybe your church or sponsoring ministry can contribute to the cost and a modest workshop fee will help cover the invitee's expenses and provide them with an honorarium.

The point is to keep growing, keep learning new ways to approach your ministry and to use it to win people to Christ. We've talked about hearing from God —- a strategy that cannot be replaced. But we must also glean from those whom God has placed in our 'space' to help us grown.

Remember, *"As iron sharpens iron, so one person sharpens another" (Proverbs 27:17, NIV).*

Looking for praise-dance conference and workshop information?

~ Visit *www.HisHemMinistry.com praise-dance blog*

"Consider Your Garments"

❧ Tip #14 ❧

Remember the last party or big dance or event you were invited to? Remember choosing the color, dress, style and shoes you were going to wear? You probably matched earrings, planned your make-up scheme and, most significantly, picked your hairstyle, <u>*waaaaay*</u> in advance of the big event.

Think about how much we honor, respect and glorify these occasions. Should not that much attention and thought be given to the garments that we wear as we minister before God?

Some of us come from church ministries that allow us budgets to purchase items on a regular basis. If we don't belong to such ministries, think about beautiful and creative ways to be able to finance a new ministry wardrobe. Could we tithe a percentage of our own personal incomes to buy a new wardrobe?

Read Exodus 28 to learn about the care ordered for the priestly garments worn by Aaron and his sons, who served before the Lord in the temple. Garments were ordered for Aaron '*that were glorious and beautiful*' (Exodus 28:2, New Living Translation).

Now ask yourself, are you not called to devote as much attention to your garments?

To afford a new garment, what if you . . .

- . . . sacrificed a month's worth of movies?
- . . . stopped buying soda or coffee and saved what you would have spent on that for a month?
- . . . hosted your own flea market or garage sale from gently used items you no longer need or use?

"Learn Your Colors"

❧ Tip #15 ☙

Let your mind wander back to a place where you felt peaceful, and safe. Let it drift back to memories about a peaceful warm day or experience you've had.

Now, I'm going to ask you to "color" that experience: If you had to color that space and time of peace, what colors would you choose? Peach, eggshell white, light green, pink, another shade of pastel?

Suppose I ask you to think of a time when you were very hyped or extremely excited about something in your life. If you had to 'color' that experience, what colors would you use? A harsh vibrant red, an electric yellow, an exuberant orange? Maybe even a tantalizing teal or turquoise?

This chapter invites you to think more deliberately about the color scheme that you use in your garments, flags, streamers and props. As you minister, think about the atmosphere you want to help set or the energy you want to emanate from your ministry presentation.

Is the song to which you're ministering talking about the 'fire' of the Holy Spirit? What colors in your dress and flags or streamers might help to perpetuate the image and atmosphere you're trying to establish? Oranges, whites, yellows and maybe even satiny whites?

Or, suppose the song or scripture you're ministering to is talking about the promises of God. In Genesis 9:12-14, we read about God's promises to never destroy the earth again by flood with His planting a bow (rainbow) in the sky and in Genesis 22:17, we read about His promise to Abraham to make him a father of many nations, which He reinforced by showing Abraham a sky filled with stars too numerous to count!

What if in our flags or garments we had representations of the rainbow or a star-filled night sky?

Know the meaning behind and use your colors!

"Accessorize: Know Your 'Praise Dance' Tools And How to Use Them"

༝ Tip #16 ༝

God has given us a wonderful wealth of instruments to use in our dance ministries: flags and streamers, tambourines, banners, scarves, billows and any number of other pageantry items.

If you don't know how to use these tools, learn. When they are used properly, these instruments and tools can be powerful weapons and awesome displays of God's Presence. For instance, 15-foot long billows, typically designed of a sheeny lamé fabric, waft elegantly and beautifully when lifted in the air by dancers holding each end, signifying the presence of God.

Once my church's dance ministry choreographed "a dance that called for a flank of flags during part of the Sha Simpson song *"He's Here In Our Midst."* When I watched that segment on DVD later, it was spiritually intense, and I was reminded of scriptures talking about flags and armies and felt onlookers also sensed God's Presence.

Learn what the Bible has to say about these instruments and when they were used and why. *Then, use them with power and anointing!*

What we learned . . .

1. Do you use flags in your ministry? Learn how to effectively use them.
2. Create a one- or two-minute choreography using a tambourine.
3. Is there a song that you *frequently* minister to that you could refresh by incorporating a new, one-minute flag (or tambourine) choreography?

   ~ *Go ahead —- give your worship tools a try!* ~

"Teach Someone Else What You Know About Praise Dance"

ॐ Tip #17 ॐ

When I was in high school, I remember helping a friend with some biology homework. While I was positioned as more of the 'expert' on the assignment, I really didn't feel that I was, but helped him anyway.

What I realized as I was helping him, and later, was that by teaching him about the assignment, I had gained a better insight into how to perform those functions.

That's one of those experiences that leads me to say once you learn a technique or step or method of dance or of using a worship tool, share that information with someone else — *for free.*

It will only enhance your ministry and, I believe, free you up to be given more information by God. It could also lead you into a deeper understanding of a subject matter, as you ponder another person's perspective or learning style.

This is the concept of the reaping and sowing: If you give freely, God will give back to you.

What we learned . . .

1. Sacrifice your time and teach someone else how to perfect or properly execute a dance move.

2. Teach . . . , so you learn better . . .

3. Expect God to replenish your well, your information source, as you 'pour into other people.'

"Know Your Spiritual Gifting"

～ Tip #18 ～

For a while when I first started publicly praise-dancing, I had many questions about why I was doing that and what I was doing. Though I enjoyed dancing, it was not an activity that I enjoyed, say, any more than roller-skating or ice-skating —- two other activities that I enjoy.

Then during a spiritual gifts Sunday School class at my church, one of my teachers, Drucilla Berry, helped me to understand that irresistible tugging in my life. She said something like, *"Your gift is not dancing (which it is not), but exhortation and encouragement!"*

As I already knew that exhortation was one of my spiritual gifts, her comment was a comforting affirmation! That affirmation and acknowledgement of that 'irresistible tugging' in that area of my life allowed me to work so much better in ministry, knowing what I was called to do and how my particular gift fit within that ministry!

Know your calling or what your spiritual gift is!

Are you a prayer warrior and able to intercede for people needing help in some area of their life? (gift of intercession)?

Are you especially gifted to be able to offer help and assistance when needed and before asked *(gifts of helps or hospitality)?*

Are you supernaturally equipped to be able to warn and direct people in how they are to move in their lives or explain to them what the Bible says *(gift of prophecy)?*

Know and <u>use</u> your spiritual gifting, in order that your ministry, church, town and area of the country may benefit!

"Practice, Practice, Practice ~ Then Practice Some More!"

∾ Tip # 19 ∾

If you are like me, you find practicing and rehearsing a choreography is one of the most challenging parts of praise dance. To me, it is a bore . . . I've come to realize, though, *a necessary bore.*

But this is so important to present a seamless ministry without bumps.

You want to practice, practice and practice —- then practice some more — so that when you present your ministry, it is so automatic that is flows right from 'rehearsed' into 'ministry.' Getting that dance and those movements into your 'spirit' is also know in the natural world as "muscle memory" —- repeating an action or movement so much that your body responds even without your seeming to think much about it.

As much as you might shoot darts with your eyes at that ministry member who 'lovingly' strong-arms the group into <u>yet one more</u> run through the choreography, respect what they are doing. Come ministry time, you will thank that person for that seemingly repetitive rehearsing.

In my own ministry, I've discovered that I really seem to "flow" in a choreography or dance after I've ministered it at least three or four times.

Also, having a set schedule to practice works better than trying to cram choreography practice in the day or night before a major presentation: each day, a little bit at a time, seals the choreography into your muscular memory.

"Think Outside the Box ~ Seek God for More Creativity"

～ Tip #20 ～

Five words into the first book of the Bible, we read of a major attribute of God: Him as <u>Creator</u>.

If that is how we first encounter Him, creating something out of nothing, ordering amazement to emerge from chaos, know that surely He can breathe and speak that same life into our little dance choreographies! We should always be seeking after Him for more creativity and a fresh approach to presenting our ministry. If we stay open to hearing Him, He will feed us with new ideas and revelations and fresh approaches to routines that perhaps we minister frequently (Jeremiah 33:3).

Is He telling you to use a certain prop, say maybe a chair that you stand on, as you stretch heavenward, to demonstrate how we are to continually look to Him for our sustenance?

Is He telling you to use a certain move, say non-traditional, to show how far, how wide, how deep is His Love for humankind?

Or, is there a certain part of your sanctuary — say the baptism pool or a loft area — that He keeps compelling you to use in your presentation? During one Palm Sunday pageantry presentation (to Israel Houghton's *"Hosanna"*), a young dancer wearing a golden angel wing cloak emerged from the empty baptism pool at the front of the church. I was in the congregation at that moment and heard the gasps and excited chatter as people suddenly realized such a 'glorious specter' had just 'emerged,' seemingly out of nowhere. *Priceless!*

You don't have to have previously seen a move that God is trying to impress upon you to do. That's the fun part: *Doing something that only He told you to do!*

Go ahead: Don't be afraid of following the Creator to breathe more creativity into your ministry dances!

"Take Care of Your Temple: Eat, Exercise and Rest Well"

❧ Tip #21 ☙

Because we are very physical before most people who watch us minister, we must do more than look 'fit' —- we must be fit. We get there by eating, exercising and resting well.

The fittest I've been in years was when I started publicly praise-dancing. Some of the garments I purchased when I initially started publicly ministering are now oversized and I am in awe of how my body changed over the years.

Because I also minister with a church-based group that dances 'live' at least three to four Sundays of the month, often 20 to 30 minutes at a time, I must be at my best, physically.

You want to be sure you look your best in your garments, minimizing all the rolls and bulges. Slenderizers can minimize a few pounds, but imagine how wonderful you'll feel when you've actually taken healthy steps to rid yourself of unwanted weight!

And that radiant face ~ don't forget that! When we take good care of our teeth, they first of all remain in our head (!) and help us have beautiful smiles *(for a lovely face that 'emotes' well, see page 28).*

Then, as we eat well, we will be radiant, as our skin has a healthy sheen, from the inside-out, and we have the stamina to dance for 15 to 20-plus minutes without looking plain tuckered out!!

Learn about health and nutrition and exercise and how your own body works. For instance, did you know that a 160-pound person can burn 219 calories and a 240-pound person 327 calories in an hour of ballroom dancing, according to The Mayo Clinic. High-impact aerobics burn 533 calories per hour (for the 160-pound person) and 796 calories for the 240-pound person).

After you have taken care of the exercise and nutrition,

don't forget to rest your body. I am not a big fan of exercise and remember the day I went to praise-dance practice, expecting to work on a dance routine, and wound up doing probably 90 minutes of Zumba® --- not my choice activity to do at that moment.

But, that night as I got ready for bed, I found that I fell asleep and slept soundly— not something that I did at night. *Wow*! I did some quick research and realized that that impact of exercise, first of all, physically tired me, but that my movements also released endorphins, which is a naturally occurring bodily hormone that helps with sleep.

So get busy: Eat well and even do one of your dance routines, once a day, which will get your heart pumping, your body moving and you healthy!

"Looking Good: Great Hygiene and Grooming"

❧ Tip #22 ☙

When we minister, we must remind ourselves that we are going before the very presence of God. We are asking Him to be in our midst, and He will be.

That being said, we must always give and present our best, which includes not only the cleanliness of our heart and soul but our physical bodies as well.

We want to look our best and we want to smell and feel our best. We must be sure that not only our physical bodies, but our garments are clean as well. A few minutes of dancing can cause perspiration that, when mixed with our dance fabrics, can magnify our body odors.

We don't want to be a stench, literally, to those before whom we minister.

We must also be sure to keep a little freshening-up kit with us so that after we minister, we can wipe away sweat and otherwise freshen up especially if we will be redressing in our street clothes to return to the sanctuary or mingle with the congregation or crowd. Baby wipes and spray-on deodorant were big with one of my ministries.

Likewise, we want to be sure we look healthy. Are our faces clean, our teeth brushed and breath fresh, our hair well-groomed? If we tend to wear heavy makeup, we might want to consider what that will look like after we have perspired a bit. If we wipe sweat from our brow or faces, will we smear our makeup? Maybe more, little or no makeup is better in this instance.

We are a representation of God and need to look our absolute best.

Remember, we always want to present a 'fresh-smelling aroma' in the spiritual and in the natural!

"Position Yourself for The Anointing"

ಞ Tip #23 ಞ

Though we dance, we do so much more than dance.

God wants us to dance to change the atmosphere of the place we're in and help others to see Him better.

I remember the time I witnessed a dance ministry truly "minister," and alter the atmosphere of the room in which we were attending the dance conference. The group was Amazing Grace Liturgical Dancers from Atlanta, and sometime later, I spoke with the leader, Kenya Griffin. What she told me was that the group spent as much time in Bible study as they did in actual physical dance practice.

Do you have private 'throne room time' with God, where you empty out yourself, but then allow Him to deposit into you? How much time do you spend in personal Bible study? We must re-organize and prioritize our days so that this happens on a daily basis . . . We must learn to hear from God. In this space, He begins to talk to us, to whisper to us about change He is preparing for the church we worship in or the ministry we work with or the people with whom we serve or work. He is anointing us, 'smearing us' with His Purpose, to do His Work.

Then, when we are so full of Him and His assignments, we go forth and serve the way He would have us to, talking, singing and otherwise ministering with our very bodies, dances and maybe even our mouths.

When we do this, He might direct us to bow before Him, as we minister a song, even if our 'right mind' tells us that's not quite the thing to do, at that time. We never know exactly what He is envisioning or why He is ordering a thing . . . our job is to just do it.

"Grow Up: Stand Taller and Stretch Longer"

∽ Tip #24 ∾

At one of my last annual physicals, my doctor recorded my height as an inch taller than I had been recording the bulk of my adult life. Mind you, I am past the age where people normally grow vertically! *How did that happen you ask?*

I'm convinced that growth was inspired by my dance teacher, Ms. Angela Graham-Williams, who stresses that, as dancers, we should pull tall our string (that imaginary line running up and down through the center of our body). When I dance, I try to remember that and am amazed that even when I feel like I'm stretching myself taller, I still feel like I can stretch just a little bit more. Ms. Angie likes to say that standing in that taller, straighter pose automatically makes you look like a dancer — even before you start *ministering!*

In turn, I tell my dance students to imagine that there are little angels on their ears, pulling the very tips of their ears *higher, higher, higher . . .*

I also think of another fellow dancer, who is always envisioned as being much taller than her 5-feet height. That is because when she dances, she stretches her limbs so much that her arms and legs actually appears to be five inches longer than they really are! She reminds me of "ElastiGirl," the character with the amazing stretching capabilities, in Disney/Pixar's 2004 *"The Incredibles."*

So even before you start to minister, look the part: Look like a dancer. *Stand taller and stretch even longer!*

What we learned . . .

1. Stand up tall: pull up that invisible string running through your body!
2. Elongate and stretch your arm and leg movements.
3. Dance gracefully . . . minister with even more grace!!

"Take a Formal Dance Class"

❧ Tip #25 ❧

Some of us came to the dance ministry because we were called here --- with and without any kind of formal training.

Sometimes, especially after many years of dancing and varied, multiple dance choreographies, our dances can start to feel and look routine, the same. *Has that ever happened to anyone but me?*

The perfect time is now, if you have not done so already, to enroll in a professional dance class. The formal training from a good teacher will help you learn basic dance techniques that will sharpen your routines and give you a new, fresh perspective on dance.

I'm reminded of a choreography that my dance ministry did; after taking an intermediate ballet course, I realized that many of the dance moves were actually basic ballet moves. One of the next times that we rehearsed that choreography and I realized one of the moves was a pique (a dance in which one foot is brought up to the knee of the other leg), I was able to clearly demonstrate it for the other dancers. Somewhere after the dance's creation, the crispness of that one particular move had been lost during the years of teaching.

So take a professional dance class: learn some new dance moves and learn to flow more creatively and crisply. Also, learn how to warm up properly, what muscles need to be stretched and in which order.

What we learned . . .

1. Learn proper ways to warm up your body, especially vulnerable areas such as the ankles, knees, neck and shoulder joints.
2. Learn some basic ballet, jazz or tap dance steps.
3. Take a professional dance class and add a layer of excellence and professionalism, to your ministry presentations!

"Minister With Passion!"

❧ Tip #26 ☙

I see some people worshipping and I wonder, 'what would she or he look like dancing?' They came to my attention because their worship seemed so pure and authentic and full of passion! Their worship was beautiful on them!

Like these authentic, beautiful worshippers, we <u>must</u> minister with passion!

If we don't, we 'project' that we could take or leave this thing we do, that we call ministry. If we feel that way, what must those that we minister before pick up from us? *Trust me, an attitude of indifference is not one you want to project!*

What am I saying here? Think about your five top activities to do: Is praise dance somewhere near the top, or at least, **<u>on</u>** that list?

Are you passionate about dancing before and for The Lord? Do people in your immediate surroundings know this, because of your passion for thinking of ways to advance the ministry and ever-more relevant ways of presenting God's message to people?

I am not suggesting that we worship the 'ministry of praise dance;' I'm hoping to say that from the wellspring of our heart, our love and honor and respect for God overflows and we want everyone to know and see that and hope that they want to *'taste and see that He is good.'*

If you are not 'passionate' about dancing before The Lord, please don't try to manufacture this: It's my experience that onlookers will see and 'sense' your insincerity.

Instead, ask God if this is indeed the ministry that He called you to minister through . . . *and if it is, pray that He will give you the passion He wants displayed!*

"You Gotta Emote!
Check Your Facial Expressions!"

∞ Tip #27 ∞

Uuugh!! Can I scream yet?

Countless times I've watched dance ministers —- *young and old* —- present beautiful choreographies, but as I look onto their faces, I 'behold' that it seems they would rather be any other place than where they are at that very moment.

Ouch! That can be such a put-down for some onlookers. If that impassioned face belongs to a child, one can wonder if a parent forced that young person to dance. If that face belongs to an adult, one can wonder if that person was dancing for God or for some other reason.

Let's not forget that our faces and our facial expressions are part of our presentation. As you work on your dance, work on emoting—showing on your face the emotions in the song or in the interpretation. *Don't look as if your body is there, but 'nobody' (dead facial expression) is home!*

One summer I taught stage presence at a dance workshop and focused on facial expressions. I remember this fantastic young dancer who had great leaps and a jazz walk and pirouettes . . . but a pitiful facial expression. I pulled her aside to tell her to work on her facial expressions; she said she would, but not till the day of the festival. Well, guess what happened on festival day? She danced beautifully, but with that same blank expression she'd worn every day of camp.

If you don't work on to emote while trying to figure out whether your left foot crosses over the right one first, you will probably forget to do it when you actually present it. Know that 'smiling' is not the only facial expression you can project: There is pain, sorrow, relief, gladness, serenity, acceptance . . . .*that funny little collection of 'emojis"? Yeah . . . consider those!*

Get ready: Em<u>ote</u>!

"*Flow ~ Just Flow . . .*"

❧ Tip #28 ☙

The dance ministry that I first joined ministered with the choir during praise and worship services on most Sundays --- *live!* This meant that we ministered to quite a few songs, with choreographies, and to quite a few, <u>without</u> choreography: We referred to those experiences without choreography as extemporaneous or impromptu . . . meaning done with no prior preparation. The music or words were whatever the Music Minister or Worship Leader decided needed to be spoken or sung into the atmosphere at that particular moment.

    For some members new to the ministry, these moments appeared to elicit the most anxious moments --- like, what do I do now? We advised them to meditate on the songs they'd been given for the week or month, but there was no guarantee that the worship leaders would not veer off into another direction without notice.

    One of the ways I learned to "flow" was to just imagine that I had a private engagement with God and was dancing before and to Him. Can you imagine what that would really look like? *To me, it'd look a lot like dancing, leading with the heart.* In my opinion, it might not include your most dramatic or complicated moves, but would simply be your purest expression of adoration and respect.

    In actuality, one of the best ways to prepare for these moments is to put on some anointed gospel or Christian music and *just dance to The Lord!*

    Begin to *flow* . . . *'just flow'!*

"Be Careful of Cutting Down Someone Else's Ministry"

❧ Tip #29 ❧

As I share this tip, I'm reminded of how the prophetess Miriam — leading one of the first Biblical references to dance that we see *(Exodus 15:20)* — was later 'dealt with' by God. The Father dealt with her after she criticized the wife of her brother, Moses, and questioned his authority as the only one to be able to hear from God *(Numbers 12: 1-16)*.

Beware that God struck her with leprosy . . . And let us stray away from any notion that God has co-signed or otherwise appointed us to somehow be judge, jury and executioner over someone else's ministry.

This especially extends to our appointed leaders, who have been given charge over us, and the Bible strongly admonishes us not to make their jobs grievous or otherwise unpleasant!

Be sure that you are breathing life into someone else's ministry —- if they ask for it, any constructive criticism can be helpful for their own ministry growth and development, but should never be demeaning and hurtful and intended to diminish, for what God calls forth, no man (or woman for that matter) will be able to stop.

Let this marinate for a minute: Imagine that every negative word you said or thought you had about someone else's ministry, God allows to 'visit' or occur in your ministry . . . *ouch! No backbiting: You don not want to experience how God might visit that same sentiment or word upon you and your ministry!*

Attempt or continue to do this, cut down or diminish someone else's ministry, and you might just wind up with your own 21st century leprosy experience!

"Fasting and Praying!"

❧ Tip #30 ❧

Imagine that you are standing in the center of a grocery store, trying to talk to a friend, whom you haven't seen in years, someone whom you just ran across . . . meanwhile, the store is remodeling and a jackhammer is going off somewhere in the distance, as a mother tries to calm an inconsolable child crying in the next aisle, as a group of chattering teen-agers keep walking past the two of you looking for items on the store shelf . . .

Now, imagine, taking away that annoying jackhammer . . . then the incessant cries of the baby . . . next those boisterous, energetic teens . . . and suddenly, you find yourself seemingly alone with your friend, able to hear her, as she explains what she's been doing in the past five years since you've seen her.

That is one of the purposes of fasting: putting us in such a position with God that we are able to more clearly 'hear' from Him and hear what He wants us to do.

As this may be a concept that is unfamiliar to you consider that other religions more routinely do this: Muslims observe a month-long sun-up to sun-down fast during their days of Ramadan.

To me, one of the most powerful scriptures in the Bible (King James Version*) clearly tells us why we need to both fast and pray — for power! In Mark 9:27 to 29, we read of Jesus telling his disciples that their work lacked power because it was apparently not linked with prayer and fasting.

(* Unfortunately, not all the versions of the Bible have this important scripture citation.)

"Avoid the Competition ~ Sidestep the Ugly!!"

❧ Tip #31 ☙

A fellow praise-dancer and I were watching a large-screen TV in our church's lobby, looking at a videotape of some visiting dancers ministering to *"Take Me to the King."*

She was watching it for the first time, and even though I'd watched part of it from a window outside the church's sanctuary, I was being amazed at how much of their dance I'd still missed because I didn't watch it head-on.

When the dance ended, another member of the church walked up to where we were standing and rather tauntingly asked, *"Seeing how much better they are than you all are?"*

Thankfully, this person did not respond, did not feed into what I consider a 'set up' to feel competitive.

The specter of competition and "good-better-best" might nip at your ministry at times. Be prepared, and best, don't fall victim to it! As a matter of fact, always endeavor to rise above it!

Avoid comparing yourself or your ministry —- or being tempted to do this —- to someone else or another ministry.

If you find yourself frequently in this position, find a relevant bit of scripture that you can meditate on as you bare your soul to God and ask Him to deliver you from that spirit. The Bible commands us to live peaceably with one another, so let's do that, putting away strife and envy.

Remember, our job is never to please man, but to always seek the pleasure of God by doing the job that we think pleases 'Him' —-and only He can be the judge of that!

~ Now What? ~
"Take It To the Streets!"

✦ Tip #32 ✦

A few years ago, I was burdened by a *"Now what?"* moment in my praise-dance experience. That urging came during a time when I served as a "Praise Dance Mama," an adult volunteer, assisting with the young praise-dance ministers at my church. I'd begun to feel unrest about the really beautiful praise-dance presentations that these young girls gave . . . **inside the church** . . . To the <u>already saved and churched</u> grandparents, parents and other family and friends!

It took me awhile to figure it out, but I know that God wanted us to put a different kind of feet on that ministry and *"take it to the streets!"*

Yes, He wanted us to take it to the streets, to evangelize through song and dance, to people in parks, juvenile homes and other juvenile detention facilities, at nursing homes, schools, parties and celebrations, family reunions, weddings, anniversary parties, parades and the like.

The Word reminds us "how beautiful are the feet of those that preach the gospel" (Isaiah 52:7)! *Yes, remember that when you 'dance,' you should be 'preaching' the gospel!*

Develop a schedule of outside-your-church-walls ministry opportunities. Learn how to evangelize and extend salvation to someone you might meet at one of these events or simply, on the streets.

Not part of your church's dance ministry or any other organized worship-arts ministry? Seek your pastor's permission to see if you can present ministry to people in these places!

Get busy for God! Take on The Great Commission, Matthew 28:16-20.

Have feet that preach! Take it to the streets!

Notes

Notes

Notes

Resources

Dancing For Him *(Lynn Hayden, founder)*
  - www.dancingforhim.com

Dancing Preachers International *(Sabrina McKenzie, founder)*
  - www.dancingpreachers.com
  - www.SabrinaMcKenzie.com

Eagles International Training Institute *(Apostle Pamela Hardy, founder)*
  - http://www.eaglesiti.org/

His Hem Ministry praise-dance blog
  - www.HisHemMinistry.com
  - https://praisedanceconferences.blogspot.com

International Christian Dance Fellowship *(inspired by Mary Jones)*
  -www.icdf.com

National Liturgical Dance Network *(Rev. Eyesha Marable, founding dir.)*
  - www.natldancenetwork.com/

Our Daily Bread *(daily Word meditation and Bible study)*
  - www.odb.org

The Praise Dance Life *(Jocelyn Richard, founder)*
  -www.thepraisedancelife.com

Bibliography

Heed. Def. intransitive verb and transitive verb. "To pay attention." "To give consideration or attention to." *Merriam-Webster.com.* http://www.merriam-webster.com/dictionary/heed. 10 April 2015 accessed.

Redemption. Def. redemption in the Bible. "The purchase back of something that had been lost, by the payment of a ransom. *Dictionary.com.* Easton's 1897 Bible Dictionary. http://dictionary.reference.com/browse/redemption. 10 April 10 2015 accessed.

"Exercise for weight loss. Calories burned in 1 hour." *Mayo Clinic.* Mayo Foundation for Medical Education and Research. http://www.mayoclinic.org/healthy-lifestyle/weight-loss/in-depth/exercise/art-20050999. 8 April 2015 accessed.

More Books from This Author
Purposed Publishing 8:18

"And A Child Shall Lead Them"
  A Practical and Spiritual Guide to Managing a Youth-Praise Dance, Mime or Worship-Arts Ministry" by Stephanie Esters

"OMG ~ I'm Praise Dancing! Now What? *A Guide Encouraging You to 'Go Ahead' and Dance" by Stephanie Ester*

~ Contact the author at hishempraise@gmail.com *~*

~ *Index* ~

Accessories, page 16

Alignment (body), page 25

Anointing, page 24

Aroma, page 23

Articulate, page 9

Backbiting, page 30

Big ('dance big'), page 10

Choreographer, page 2

Clothes, page 14

Colors, page 15

Competition, page 32

Conference, page 13

Creativity, page, 20

Creator, page 20

Dance, pages 10, 26

Delayed obedience, page 3

Development (ministry development), page 13

Disobedience, page 3

Eli, page 5

Emote, page 28

Evangelism, page 33

Exodus 28 (garments), page 14

Facial expressions, page 28

Fasting, page 31

Fitness, page 21

Flags, page 20

Flow, page 29

Garments, page 14

God, pages 1-3, 5

Grace, page 7

Health, page 21

Heed, page 3

Hope, page 7

Hubris (pride), page 6

Humbleness, page 6

Humility, page 10

Hygiene, page 23

Iron, page 13

Leprosy, page 30

Listen, page 3

Living honorably, page 5

Love, page 7

Lyrics, page 4

Mercy, page 7

Minister, pages 8, 27

Ministering, page 8, 27

Miriam, page 30

Muscle memory, page 19

'Now What?,' page 33

Nutrition, page 21-22

Obedience, page 3

Passion, page 27

Performing, page 8

Posture, page 25

Practice, page 19

Prayer, page 31

Redemption, page 7

Rest, page 21

Sacrifice, page 7, 14

Salome, page 11

Salvation, page 7

Seduction, page 11

Seeking (seek after God), page 1

Self-critique, page 12

Sexiness (in praise dance), page 11

Sin, page 7

Smell, page 23

Spiritual gifts, page 18

Stench, page 23

Street, page 33

Stretch, page 25

Tambourines, page 16

Teaching, pages 17, 23

Temple (body), page 21

Themes (Biblical themes), page 7

Tools (worship tools), page 16

Videotape, page 12

Williams, Angela Graham, page 25

Workshop, page 13

www.ingramcontent.com/pod-product-compliance
Lightning Source LLC
LaVergne TN
LVHW051513070426
835507LV00022B/3080